Shakespeare, Live!
2

by
Michelle Lang

Shakespeare, Live!

2

Copyright © 2019 by Michelle Lang

Created in 2000 by Michelle Lang

ISBN: 978-1-7322636-9-7

Edited by Deborah M. Lang

Published by RBL PUBLISHING

Dedication

To my parents.

Thank you for allowing my creativity to fly.

(Again.)

The world premiere of Shakespeare, Live! 2
was performed in Eau Claire, Wisconsin and toured
libraries, theatres, and festivals in the mid-west.
Directed by Michelle Lang.
Produced by Deborah Lang.

@TheMichelleLang | @RelaxationBasedLifestyle

NOTES

The show is approximately 50 minutes without an intermission.

The cast must interact with the audience. Each actor should be trained on how to improve and find comedy from authentic moments created by the audience.

When the characters ask the audience a question, they need to get an answer from the audience. Pauses for their responses are not written in but should be executed during production.

CHARACTERS

Shakespeare
Witch #1
Witch #2
Witch #3
Veronica
Katherine
Lady Macbeth
Calpurnia
Mercutio
Little Witch

All roles can be cast as male or female.

SETTING THE STAGE

The set is a large "box" made with PCP pipes and a blue sheet hung from each side as a "curtain." The box should be about 6 feet tall by 8 feet wide and 3 feet deep. All the actors use the box as "back-stage." On the front it says, "Shakespeare, Live!" The blue "box" can be easily torn down and transported to parks, libraries, and various locations.

In the center of the stage is a large cauldron. The pot is 2D, but it's painted to look as if it's 3D. The pot must be large enough that cast members can fit behind it and be completely hidden.

SHAKESPEARE, LIVE!

2

A play in one act

MUSIC BEGINS ten minutes before curtain call.

Five minutes before curtain call, Veronica enters like a "normal" audience member and sits with the children. Three Witches meander around the stage and into the audience searching for items to add to their stew. As they find things (wadded Kleenex, candy wrappers, etc…) they bring them to stage and toss them in the pot.

MUSIC ENDS.

The Witches start the show by chanting/dancing around the pot. The Witches speak with a 4/4 count. There is an emphasis on the 1st and 3rd beats. (Note: This is a norm, but not a rule. Some lines do not have the rhythm. The Witches also ab-lib with the audience, and those conversations do not need to have the 4/4 count.)

ALL 3 WITCHES:	Round and round and round we go up and down, high and low. Futures, YOUR futures are what we know!
Witch #1:	Let's tell them!
Witch #2:	Not yet!
Witch #1:	Patience, my dear.
Witch #2:	We know things they are not to hear.
Witch #3:	To hear?
Witch #2:	To hear?
Witch #1:	Not yet! Shhhhhhhhh!
ALL 3:	Round and round and round we go up and down, high and low. Futures, your futures are what we know!
Witch #3:	Let's tell them!
Witch #2:	Not Yet!
Witch #1:	Patience, my dear.
Witch #2:	We know things they are not to hear.

Witch #3:   To hear?

Witch #2:   To hear?

Witch #1:   Not yet!

The Witches stop dancing.

Witch #2:   You know, we need something for this
               new sneezing spell.

Witch #1:   You're right…it is just not looking well.

Witch #3:   Maybe one of the kids could tell! What
do we need to make this sneezing stew work? Any
ideas?

*The Witches get the audience to give suggestions for the stew:
toads, spiders, ants…etc…Eventually, Veronica pipes up.*

Veronica: A bat.

Witch #3:   A bat?

Witch #2:   A brat? *(Pronounced "brought"…as in the
hotdog-ish food item.)*

Witch #1:   A BRAT? *(As in a naughty child.)*

Witch #1/#2: THAT'S IT! We forgot to add a brat!

Witch #3:   Oh, NO! Anything but that! Last time we added a child she RUINED the entire sum!

Veronica: All three of you sure are dumb.

The Witches turn to Veronica, a gleam in their eyes.

Witch #2:   It seems like we have a volunteer!

Witch #1:   Why don't you come over here?

Veronica: Why should I?

ALL 3:   You will get your fortune told!

The three Witches lean forward and bat their eyelashes. Veronica shrugs.

Veronica: Okay.

Veronica skips to the stage. The Witches twitter and giggle with shrouded excitement. Witch #1 and #2 grab one of her hands. Witch #3 snags the other. They inspect her palms as if they are reading her fortune.

Witch #1:   Shows here…pretty soon you will be in a warm place…

Witch #2:   a very warm place

Witch #1:   called Honolulu…

Witch #3:   Honolulu?

Witch #1:   Nope, I was wrong.

ALL 3:   Looks like you will be dissolving in a
sneezing stew!

They lift Veronica and place her in the pot.

Veronica: **AHHH-CHEWWWWW!**

*The sneeze sends Veronica down, hiding. The Witches dance
around the pot.*

ALL 3:   Round and round and round we go
              up and down, high and low.

Veronica: *(While they say "up and down, high and
              low" Veronica pops up)*
              I HATE YOU GUYS.

ALL 3:   No, no, no!

Witch #1:   You get back down in there.

Witch #2:   Your ideas are not wanted here!

Veronica hides in the pot.

ALL 3:   **SHHHHHHH!!!**

The Witches stop dancing. Beat.

Witch #3:   What are we to do today?

Witch #1:   I hear Shakespeare is scheduled to come
this way!

Witch #2:   Really?

Witch #3:   Shakespeare?

Witch #2:   Here?

Witch #2/#3: WITH US?!?

Witch #1:   Not WITH us. He doesn't know we're
here.

Witch #2:   DOESN'T KNOW WE'RE HERE?

Witch #3:   Oh, dear.

Veronica: *(popping up)* I have a good idear!

ALL 3:   Your idears are not wanted here.
SHHHHHH!

Witch #3:   Let's cast a spell so he knows we're here!

Witch #2:   Now that is a good idear.

ALL 3:   Round and round and round we go
up and down, high and low.
Futures, your futures are what we know -

Veronica: *(popping up)* I HATE THIS SHOW!

ALL 3:   No, no, no! *(With each "no" Veronica goes lower into the pot.)*

Witch #1:   Your comments are not wanted here.

Witch #3:   *(To #1)* I told you we shouldn't have put a brat *(food)* in there!

Witch #2:   It is not a brat *(food)* it is a BRAT *(child)* you hear?

Witch #3:   Brat *(food)* brat *(child)*…they are spelled the same.

Witch #2:   You are so incredibly lame. A brat *(food)* tastes good, and a BRAT *(child)* is usually SPOILED.

Veronica pops up and sticks out her tongue, then hides again.

Witch #2:   My point, exactly.

Witch #1:   We needed something annoying for our new sneezing spell. It is not my fault she always has something obnoxious to tell.

Witch #2:   And it is not my fault she's not dissolving well.

Witch #1:   Let's just continue with Shakespeare's spell.

Veronica: *(pops up)* Who is Shakespeare?

The three Witches GASP.

Witch #1: Who is Shakespeare?

Witch #2: Who is Shakespeare?

Witch #3: Who is Shakespeare?

Shakespeare: *(from backstage)* I AM SHAKESPEARE!

ALL 3:   AHHH! He's here!

The Witches hide, but stay on stage. Shakespeare enters.

Shakespeare: I am Shakespeare! I have stepped into the modern world to show you some of my most famous characters! But first, you need to tell me something about someone very, very, very, very, important. ME! So, what do you know about SHAKESPEARE?

Shakespeare gets the audience to tell him facts about himself. If the audience doesn't know any, he can play guessing games; for example, "How many brothers and sisters did I have?" Someone will, eventually, guess five, and Shakespeare will be impressed at their knowledge about his life. Feel free to use any facts like: Shakespeare was born in Stratford Upon Avon, his dad was John, his mom was Mary. His dad made gloves. He married a woman named Anne Hathaway, who was 18 years older than him. He worked in London at the Globe...etc...

Veronica: *(pops up)* Wow Mr., you sure do have a big head! *(hides)*

Shakespeare: Who just said I work with lead? No, I did not work with lead! Back in MY day, we didn't have those fancy little pencils full of lead with the clicky-clicky back and an eraser on the end. And do you know why we didn't have erasers? Because SHAKESPEARE never makes mistakes!

Veronica: *(pops up)* You are a very conceited man! *(hides)*

Shakespeare: No, no, no! I never cooked SPAM! Who is saying all these dreadful things?

The audience may respond. If so, play along. Shakespeare can look in the pot if need be, but pretend not to see anything. Continue the game of "hide and go seek" with Veronica popping up and down a few times.

Shakespeare: Well, I think that is enough of that. Clearly, someone is playing tricks on me. Not to worry, I am un-trickable. And now it's time to show you pictures of my most famous characters! The photos are safely hidden in my trunk. No one will EVER find them.

The Witches "freeze" Shakespeare.

Witch #1:   What fun!

Witch #2 :   Let's steal Shakespeare's photos!

Witch #3:   But why!

Witch #2:   Why? Why? Why not!

Witch #3:   Good point. Who will get them?

Witch #2:   Not ME!

Witch #3:   Not me!

Witch #1:   Hey, Little Witch!

Little Witch peeks out from behind the box.

Little Witch: OH, GEE!

Witch #1:   You want to be a witch like us, right?

Little Witch: Yes, no…I mean, I might!

Witch #2:   In that case, we have a task for you.

Little Witch: Boo, hoo! Don't make me eat another
stinky shoe.

The Witches scoff.

Witch #1:   We wouldn't do something like…that.

Witch #2:   US? Never.

Witch #1 wraps her arm around Little Witch's shoulder.

Witch #1:   Of COURSE NOT, Little Witch.

Witch #2:   We just need you to get Shakespeare's photos! They are hidden in his trunk.

Witch #3:   See? It's an easy task for you to do!

ALL 3:   Now, SHOO!

Little Witch: AHHHHHH!

Little Witch scurries off. The Witches un-freeze Shakespeare.

Shakespeare: The three women characters I am going to show you are beautiful: Lady Macbeth, Katherine, and Calpurnia. They are all stunning, but like most women they have their downfalls.

ALL 3:   *(Angrily)* Ohhhhh.

Witch #1:   He's stuck in the past! You can't say stuff like that anymore!

The Witches grumble, upset at Shakespeare's faux macho-ism.

Shakespeare: Lady Macbeth is too bossy and demanding. Katherine is too shrewd, and Calpurnia worries way toooooo much for her own good. I would have brought them in person, but I think they have a crush on me. AH, but who can blame them?

The Witches freeze Shakespeare.

Witch #1:   This Shakespeare character is making me sick.

Witch #2:   I agree! Let's cast a spell on him!

Witch #3:   The sneezing spell! Go!

ALL 3:   Round and round and round we go
up and down, high and low.
A cold, A COLD placed in your nose.
Makes you sneeze whenever it blows!

The Witches un-freeze Shakespeare.

Shakespeare: AHHHHH chew! Excuse me! Phew! What a sneeze! I will be right back. I will get the photos. And a tissue.

Shakespeare swaggers behind the box. Little Witch enters from the opposite side.

Little Witch: I got them! I got them! I found them in a trunk!

Witch #1:   Good job Little Witch.

ALL 3:   Now SHOOO!

Little Witch: AHHHHHHH

Witch #2:   Let's bring the photos to life!

Witch #3:   How are we going to do that?

Witch #1:   Perhaps we can…sit on 'em?

Witch #2:   Hatch 'em like a baby chick!

Witch #1 and #2 drop the photos and rub their butts all over them. Witch #2 gets another idea.

Witch #2:   OR we can rub them! Like a magic lamp.

Witch #2 raises one up and rubs it…anxiously waiting for a genie to pop out.

Witch #3:   Maybe the audience has a better idea.

Witch #3 asks the audience. Eventually the answer should be "CAST A SPELL!"

Witch #1:   A spell?

Witch #2:   A SPELL?

Witch #3:   So obvious.

ALL 3:   WE LOVE IT!

Witch #2:   Here we go! Say it with us if you know it!

The Witches hold Calpurnia's photo up and hover it over the pot.

ALL 3:   Round and round and round we go
                Up and down, high and low.

Witch #1:   It's Calpurnia

Witch #2:   Calpurnia

Witch #3:   Calpurnia's show.

ALL 3:   So tell us, Calpurnia, what you know!

The Witches drop the photo into the pot.

Calpurnia rises out of the pot. MUSIC BEGINS.
(Suggestion: Symphony No. 40 in G minor, K. 550:1. Allegro
Malto by Mozart.)

Calpurnia: I am Calpurnia. Wife of the magnifi-
cent Julius Caesar. My husband could have been king
if he had wanted to. One night, I had this awful dream
that my husband was going to be killed. I told him he
should not go out, but he refused to listen to anything I
said. "Don't go! Don't go! Caesar, what about my awful
dream?" I asked. "You could be killed out there today!
Stay home with me!" He refused to listen and went out
to be crowned as king, calling my fears foolish! "See
how foolish your fears seem now, Calpurnia," he said.
Well, my dear husband never came back. SO, let this be
a lesson to all you! Listen to your wives! For what they
speak is true!

MUSIC ENDS

Veronica: *(Still in the pot)* That was fun!

Witch #3: Yah! Let's do another one! Who should we do next? Katherine or Lady Macbeth?

They hold Katherine's photo over the pot.

ALL 3: Round and Round and Round we go
up and down, high and low

Witch #1: It's Katherine

Witch #2: Katherine

Witch #3: Katherine's show.

ALL 3: So tell us, Katherine, what you know!

The Witches drop the photo in.

Katherine rises up from the pot. MUSIC BEGINS.
(Suggestion: Coriolan Overture, Op. 62) Katherine moves around the audience, pausing dramatically as the music pauses. The monologue only lasts about a minute and a half. The last line, "As silly as it may seem, it turned out alright," happens as the music shifts into the "nicer" variation.

Katherine: I am Katherine…also known as Katherine the SHREW! That means I'm not very nice. Let me tell you a story. I come from a household where my sister is very beautiful, and I am not. Well, it came time when my beautiful sister, Bianca, wanted to get married. But, me, being the older sister my dad said I would have to get married first. But no one wants to marry Katherine the SHREW! Well, eventually, a man as shrew as myself came in and married me. He took me home, and after a lot of fuss, he taught me how to cook and clean and obey as every "good" wife should do. The sun was only out if he said it was out. And the moon was out, even if it was daylight. As silly as it may seem, it turned out alright.

MUSIC ENDS

Veronica: That one was the best!

Witch #3:   Let's bring alive the rest!

Witch #1:   You ready to do Lady Macbeth?

The Witches hold Lady Macbeth's photo over the pot.

ALL 3:   Round and round and round we go
              up and down high and low!

Witch #1:   It's Lady Macbeth

Witch #2:   Lady Macbeth

Witch #3:   Lady Macbeth's show.

ALL 3:   So tell us, Lady Macbeth, what you
know!

Lady Macbeth rises from the pot. MUSIC BEGINS. (Suggestion Symphony No. 3 in E-Flat Major, Op. 55 "Eroica") The portion where the music grows increasingly loud should be where Lady Macbeth tells the audience to applaud for their queen (At about 40 seconds into the song.)

Lady Macbeth:I am lady Macbeth. My husband got told by witches that he would soon be king of the land…and that would make me the queen of the land. I told Macbeth all he would have to do is kill the current king. "Screw your courage to the sticking place" is all you have to do! But Macbeth, being the wuss that he is, refused to do what I told him to do. Eventually, I gave him enough courage to kill that old king! And that made me the queen of the land! *(to the audience)* Well, applaud! Clap for your queen! You are looking at Lady Macbeth! Don't stop clapping! Louder! MORE! Don't you realize who I am *(etc…)* Okay, enough." Well, things went from bad to worse. I started having nightmares, and Macbeth went a little insane. Pretty soon, a huge army attacked us and my poor husband's head got cut off — sob, sob, sob.

Witch #3:   Ah man…I hate it when people start to cry.

Veronica: Yah, meeee tooo.

Witch #1:   Come on, let's fly.

Witch #2:   Goodbye.

The Witches leave.

Veronica: Hey, what about me??? Hey witches? It is toasty in here. AH CHEW!

The sneeze sends Veronica back into the pot. Calpurnia saunters to Lady Macbeth.

Calpurnia: Hey, what is wrong? Oh, don't wipe your nose on your sleeve…germs.

Katherine: Toughen up! It could be worse…at least you don't have a perfect sister. That is the worst. All the expectations to live up to all the time.

Calpurnia: At least your husband didn't get murdered right before he was crowned king.

Lady Macbeth: My husband's head was put on a spear.

Calpurnia: Oh. *(uneasy silence)* So, did you hear about the bubonic plague?

Katherine: Calpurnia, stop trying to change the subject.

Calpurnia: Sorry. Limbs are falling off. For reals.

Katherine: Don't you know what year we are in? This is era of female empowerment and women superheroe movies. We can't just sit here and sob about our lives.

Lady Macbeth:*(sob)* Do you have a better idea?

Katherine:　　What do you usually do when you get sad?

Calpurnia:　　I clean!

Lady Macbeth: *(Sob)* I don't want to clean!

Katherine:　　Me either. Maybe the audience can help us out! What do you do when you are sad?

The audience gives suggestions. (Adults can answer too.) Eventually, try to get someone to say they talk to someone.

Katherine:　　We could talk to someone! You know what? I bet Shakespeare would speak with us…he is such a nice, handsome man. *(sigh)*

Calpurnia:　　He is sooooo dreamy! Maybe I could talk him into writing me a sonnet!

Shakespeare enters. He sees the women and ducks.

Katherine:　　You know…I bet if I asked really sweetly, he would change my sister into a rat or something.

Witch #2 glides out from behind the box. She flutters her arms at Shakespeare.

Shakespeare:　　AHHHHH CHHHHHEWWW!

Lady Macbeth: What was that?

Calpurnia: It is Shakespeare! I can recognize his sinus expulsions from a mile away. He's plague free. I can tell.

Katherine: He is soooo dreamy!

Calpurnia: Do you think he would give me an autograph?

Katherine: Perhaps, but we have to catch him first!

Lady Macbeth: Get him!

MUSIC BEGINS. The characters start a choreographed chase scene through the audience. The kids should yell and cheer…either trying to help Shakespeare or the girls. The characters can ad-lib the scene: for example: "Don't tell them where I am! Hide me! etc… The three women end up behind the box. Shakespeare ends alone on stage. MUSIC ENDS.

Shakespeare: Phew! I think I lost them! Just in case…I have a sword to fend them off! Ungar!

The Witches pop out from various places, mocking the three women's voices.

Witch #1: You hoooo!

Shakespeare jumps at each "tease" from the Witches as they come out of hiding and then disappear again.

Witch #2:   Over here!

Witch #3:   Shakespeare!

Witch #2:   Over here, handsome!

Shakespeare: AHHHH! I am the most talented man alive! Yes! The most talented –

The Witches freeze him.

Witch #1:   Hummm…the most talented? We'll see about that! I think it's time to knock Shakespeare down a few notches! I need a volunteer. A talented-

They un-freeze Shakespeare long enough to get the next word out.

Shakespeare: STRONGEST-

They freeze him again.

Witch #1:   strong -

They un-freeze him.

Shakespeare: AND POWERFUL!

Witch #1:   and powerful volunteer.

This time, they leave him unfrozen.

Witch #1:   Shakespeare, because you are so powerful, I will let you choose some of your characters to
wage war against. We will end this here and now. Dis-
cern who is the strongest and most powerful. YOU or
your CHARACTERS.

Shakespeare: Of course, I would be delighted.

*The Witches give Shakespeare name-tags for around the audience
member's neck to mark them as different characters from his plays.
Shakespeare meanders through the audience, looking for volunteers
to "wage war against."*

Shakespeare: I will beat my good friend Romeo. You
look like you're a love-struck kind of fellow.

Shakespeare picks a child to play Romeo.

Shakespeare: And I will like to go against someone
dead already. Perhaps the ghost of Hamlet's father…

*Shakespeare chooses a "dead father" volunteer. (An ADULT for
this role.)*

Shakespeare: And I really like fairies, how about Titania, the queen of all fairies? You? Perfect.

Shakespeare finds his "Titania."

Shakespeare: Now one more…how about big mean
Claudius. I need a man who looks like he is evil enough
to put poison in someone's ear. Someone truly wicked
and cruel.

Shakespeare meanders through the crowd, glaring at the men and women in the audience…attempting to pick someone he thinks looks the, "meanest of them all." He ends on a sweet looking young girl or boy. All the chosen volunteers line up on stage. (Note: The Witches help Shakespeare organize and wrangle the audience members.)

Witch #1: Mercutio will be your leader, I should mention…So listen up! Pay attention!

Mercutio enters from behind the box.

Mercutio: Alright, everyone, listen up! This is WAR! TUG OF WAR! Now, I need all of you, including YOU *(the audience)*, to do warm-ups with me. First, get that neck going.

Mercutio leads the entire audience in all sorts of crazy warm-ups. Examples: finger stretches, ear pulls, tongue extensions, knuckle cracking, etc…

Mercutio: *(To the characters on stage.)* Alright team …I have a strategy…all you need to do is follow along with me. If I yell, "forward," you go forward…if I yell, "back,"…we all go back. Forward means forward. Back means back. Not very complicated, but in the heat of battle, your brain gets all scrambled. You got it?

Volunteers: GOT IT!

Mercutio: LOUDER!

Volunteers: GOT IT!!!

Mercutio: LOUDER!!!

Volunteers: GOTTT ITTTTT!

Mercutio holds his hands to his ears.

Mercutio: You trying to blow out my eardrum? No need to yell, I'm standing right here!

Mercutio turns to Shakespeare.

Mercutio: Alright, Shakespeare! We will turn you into worm's meat!

Shakespeare: Why, you are nothing but a stock-fish! A dried neat's-tongue. A three-inch fool!

Mercutio: Go, prick thy face, thou lily-livered man!

Shakespeare: Any more of your weak conversating will infect my brain. Let's battle!

Mercutio: You poisonous bunch-backed toad. Let's DO THIS!

MUSIC BEGINS.
(Suggested music: Verdi Requiem, Dies Irae.)

NOTE: In order to contain the pulling have a bungee cord tied into the middle of the tug of war rope. This will enable Shakespeare to have movement freedom without being pulled off stage. The tug of war should be comedic and choreographed. The Witches act as referees. Veronica calls out "Round #1…go!" and "Round #2… go!" etc…The audience should cheer. Shakespeare's pulling is more of a comedy act as he gets yanked and flung all over the stage.

At the final moment of the tug of war, the Witches make Shakespeare sneeze, which causes him to lose.

Shakespeare: **AHHHHHCHEEEEEWWWW!**

Shakespeare falls flat on his face. MUSIC ENDS.

Mercutio: HAHA! We did it! We are the winners! Let's give Romeo, Ghost, Claudius, and Titania a hand! Wonderful job!

The audience claps for the volunteers.

Shakespeare: That's not fair! I sneezed! Loss by sinus tingles! Wait, come back here all of you! Oh! A curse on all your houses!

Witch #1: Well, Shakespeare…it looks like you lose!

Shakespeare: Not fair! Shakespeare never loses! I demand a re-match! This time I will not…Ahhhhhhh chew! Whew!

Witch #2:   You will not what?

Shakespeare: I will not...AHHHHH CHHHEEEW-
WWWW!

Witch #3:   It looks like our spell works...despite the
spoiled brat.

Veronica: Why do you keep calling me that?

Shakespeare: Spell, what spell?

Witch #1:   SHHHHH nobody tell!

Veronica: They cast a spell on you to make you
sneeze!

Shakespeare: Can they do that?

Witch #2:   We can do anything we please!

Shakespeare: You have made me look like a fool in
front of all these people! I demand revenge! I challenge
you to a man to witch sword fight! UNGAR!

Witch #1:   We do not use violence, Shakespeare.
Don't you know what era you are in?

*Shakespeare shifts his sword, pointing it from one Witch to the
other.*

Shakespeare Neither do I!

MUSIC BEGINS.

Shakespeare lunges at Witch #1, missing her. He dives for Witch #2. The Witches are too fast and magical for him. He heaves around, attempting to rid himself of the Witches.

Calpurnia, Katherine, and Lady Macbeth enter part way through the fight, Shakespeare is on the ground, surrounded by the Witches. They have him in a spell, captured in a "bubble" in the middle of them. Shakespeare bangs on the "walls" and mimes being "trapped."

Calpurnia: AHHHHH! There is Shakespeare!

Katherine: He looks like he is in a muddle! Or he's practicing mime-ry.

Lady Macbeth: If we don't help him, he is going to end up like my husband!

Katherine: Should we help him?

Calpurnia: Of course we should help him! Or how will I ever get my sonnet?

Lady Macbeth: It looks like the only way to stop the witches is to beat them at their own game.

Calpurnia: I don't know how to sword fight!

Lady Macbeth: No, no. I mean, we have to come up with a spell.

The ladies look at each other with confusion. Do you know magic? Do you? Spell, spell what? You should know magic. No, why should I?...Then they turn to audience...

Calpurnia: Hey! Do YOU know some spells?

Lady Macbeth:What have the witches been chanting?

Katherine: Have you heard anything?

The audience should say, "Round and round and round we go, up and down high and low."

Katherine: Perfect! Now we need to come up with the last few lines to free Shakespeare.

Lady Macbeth:What rhymes with "go" and "low"?

The audience answers snow...blow...so...etc...the three girls have to come up with a rhyme using the words the audience suggests.

Katherine: We all need to do magic arms. Whatever feels magical to you.

Calpurnia begins to shake and gyrate. She looks like the inflatable "man" outside of a used car dealership. The other two stare at her.

Lady Macbeth How does she do that?

Katherine She's so...active.

Katherine: At the end of the spell, the Witches will run away. Let's practice!

Calpurnia stops moving and catches her breath as the other two lead the audience to say the chant several times.

Katherine: How many times should we say it?

The audience answers. The girls use whatever reasonable number they say.

Lady Macbeth: Okay, on the count of three. Ready? One, two, three! Magic hands, let's shake it!

The girls and the audience all stand and shake like maniacs.

ALL: Round and round and round we go
                up and down, high and low
                " . . . . . . "
                " . . . . "

Katherine: KEEP CHANTING!!!! And shaking!

The audience continues wiggling and chanting the magic words.

The Witches begin to "blow" around the stage. They are "pulled" by "magical forces" behind the box. Shakespeare is saved! Veronica topples out of the pot, free at last.

Veronica: Thank you, Shakespeare, you saved my life!

Shakespeare: What can I say? I am just really good.

Katherine: SHAKESPEARE!!!

The three women rush to Shakespeare, their arms are outstretched, their lips pursed. Shakespeare freezes them.

Shakespeare: *(to Veronica)* Now, I need your to help to help me turn these women back into photographs! I saved your life, you save mine. Got any good ideas? I've been suffering from writer's block recently.

Veronica: Whenever I want my mommy to do something for me all I have to do is ask really, really nicely. But I can't do it alone. I need everyone in the audience to help. I need everyone to say, "Please, pretty please!"

ALL: Please, pretty please!

The three women stay frozen, still in their "flesh and blood" form.

Veronica: Oh, no! It didn't work. Maybe we really need to heap it on. Louder everyone!

ALL: PLEASE, PRETTY PLEASE!

The characters stay frozen.

Veronica: It's STILL not working! *(Outloud, to herself)*Think Vivi-pod, THINK! What do I do when I really, really, really want something. *(She gets another idea and turns to the audience.)* Say it with me again but this time pout your lip like this!

ALL: PLEASE! PRETTY PLEASE!!!

Katherine spins into the pot. She flings her photograph out.

Veronica: It's working! Let's add some eyelash bat-
ting.

ALL: "PLEASE! PRETTY PLEASE!!!"

*Lady Macbeth and Calpurnia both twirl into the pot and toss out
their photographs.*

Veronica: It WORKED! We did it!

Shakespeare: Wow, Veronica. Thanks a lot!
AMAZING! Hey, that asking really nice stuff is highly
effective. *(To the audience)* All of you can do that kind of
magic at home and see if it works. Just don't tell your
parents it is magic, okay? It is our little secret!

Shakespeare and Veronica bow and exit behind the box.

END OF PLAY

Discover more books from RBL PUBLISHING

A MERMAID'S GUIDE:
Empower Your Child in Water and in Life.

A Mermaid's Guide is a modern, holistic swim method focused on
turning every child into a safe, joyful swimmer.
(Starting in the bathtub.)

Written by Michelle Lang, graduate of the WSI (Water Safety
Instructor) Red Cross course and swim instructor to the stars,
A Mermaid's Guide is your new, must-have parenting book.

**Get your copy today on Amazo.com | Barnes & Noble
Audible, Hardcover, Paperback, Kindle**

Where the Sanity Ends

*Hilarious and touching, "Where the Sanity Ends" is a comedic parody
of Shel Silverstein's, "Where The Sidewalk Ends" for parents with
toddlers. Best selling author and award-winning actress Michelle Lang
inscribes humorous prose about important topics like how to smuggle
cold brew through airport security, the dearth of lactating men, and
the sexy woes of using reusable diapers.*

*Deliciously Illustrated by artist Holli Jacobson, Where The Sanity
Ends makes a perfect gift for every parent.*

Get yours on Amazon.com

Under the Rug

Join Andy on a quest to discover the TRUTH about what is under the rug. Is it leeches? Cockroaches? Or something far more disgusting?

Under the Rug is entertainment sprinkled with unique vocabulary words, alluring alliteration, and energizing illustrations to help every child fall in love with reading.

Bubble

A pure, peaceful bubble, soars through the sky to see what it can discover. Along the way, Bubble meets other bubbles who influence how Bubble looks and feels. Will Bubble stay the clear bubble it once was or become a different bubble all together?

Bubble is a story about how other people touch our lives long after they are gone.

Toddy the Dot

There was once a dot named Toddy. Toddy knew a lot of other dots existed, but Toddy still felt very alone. All the other dots were part of shapes. Shapes that fit perfectly together. Every day Toddy wandered from shape to shape, hoping to find a place to fit in.

Toddy the Dot is a story about how to navigate negative emotions and make friends.

@TheMichelleLang | @RelaxationBasedLifestyle

www.ingramcontent.com/pod-product-compliance
Lightning Source LLC
Chambersburg PA
CBHW021148020426
42331CB00005B/959